T0381421

Gathered Thoughts

Radical Candor

Valen Hart

Print information available on the last page.

Rev. date: 09/24/2018

To order additional copies of this book, contact:
Xlibris
1-888-795-4274
www.Xlibris.com
Orders@Xlibris.com

Gathered Thoughts

Curated by Valen Hart

Radical Candor
Quotes, Questions and Phrases

Words have a unique capacity to inspire and motivate, to resonate with our experiences, and to elicit fervent emotion. Stretch your mind, ponder another's ideas, and share your insights. Start a conversation that will stimulate you, even challenge your beliefs. Instead of placating to what is comfortable, you may be surprised how articulating your thoughts to others and absorbing theirs can greatly elevate your intellect.

On My Mind – Megan James

It's better to be quiet and
thought a fool than to speak
and remove all doubt

Lincoln

Decision is risk rooted in the
courage of being free

Tillich

You either loathe the wicked
or imitate them.

Oscar Wilde

He who angers you,
conquers you.

Elizabeth Kinney

Seek respect, not attention. It
lasts longer.

Ziad Abdelnour

In the end, people tend to
regret inaction the most.

T. Gilovich

No one can make you
feel inferior without your
consent.

- Eleanor Roosevelt

Surrender – Megan James

No one heals himself by
hurting another.

Saint Ambrose

Silence provides many
answers.

We rebel only to find
ourselves in the midst of
the familiar.

Exhale then give others
permission to as well.

We tend to ignore the
yellow lights in life.

Kick the drug of
certainty.

Nobody truly interesting
is universally liked.

Time gallops on regardless of your mood.

Freedom trumps all yet only health allows one to enjoy it.

Justifying is our default system.

Hubris to humility is an impossible journey for some.

Unrealistic expectations are the embryos for disappointment.

Everyone has a blind spot.

There is often tension between interest in beauty and repulsion of vanity.

Avoid flattery, that's easier said than done.

Strong Shoulders – Megan James

We are what we
pretend to be.

Kurt Vonnegut

Know your audience.

Being alone has power.

What you feel deep down
in your heart is your own
business.

There is such a thing as
loyal to a fault.

During the ascension into affluence, ones integrity may falter and possibly end up on trial.

Reason from first principals.

Elon Musk

Stumbling blocks are temporary.

It's tricky to catch yourself during a free fall.

Underestimate me. That will be fun.

When I travel, I pack my sarcasm. It weighs a ton.

Your audacity is astonishing.

Should I go ahead and pretend not to notice what you may be inferring?

Sophia - Lisset DeVal

Know when to ask for more.

When you're not sure what
to land on, hit pause.

If you always do what
interests you, at least one
person is pleased.

-Katherine Hepburn

Diplomacy is doing the
worst in the best possible
way.

The appetite for novelty cuts the thirst for knowledge.

Seek your own form of validation.

Being one's confidante isn't easy.

Don't be afraid to give up the good for the great.

John D Rocksefeller

Find room to be different.

Learn the art of shapeshifting.

Keep the door of possibilities
wide open.

Creativity is intelligence
having fun.

-Albert Einstein

We are never left with nothing,
as long as we have the freedom
to choose how we respond.

The truth of another may not resonate at first.

Love is the irresistible desire to be irresistibly desired.

-Robert Frost

Natasha - Lisset DeVal

In the end, marriage boils
down to surviving each other's
peculiar idiosyncrasies.

Intimacy creates
understanding and
understanding creates love.

Anais Nin

There was no daylight
between us.

Mystery leaves space for
growth.

Love people and use stuff.
Don't use people and love stuff.

Let there be spaces in your togetherness.

You're a paradox waiting to happen.

Love is a feeling that can't be manufactured.

Do you have any
idea who
I think I am?

Valentina – Lisset DeVal

Everyone
you will ever
meet knows
something
you don't.

- Bill Nye

Midlife and adolescence
are the periods in life when
everything seems to be in
the wrong size.

Middle age crept in
stealth like a cat.

They say "you'll
understand when you're
older". I'm older... still
waiting.

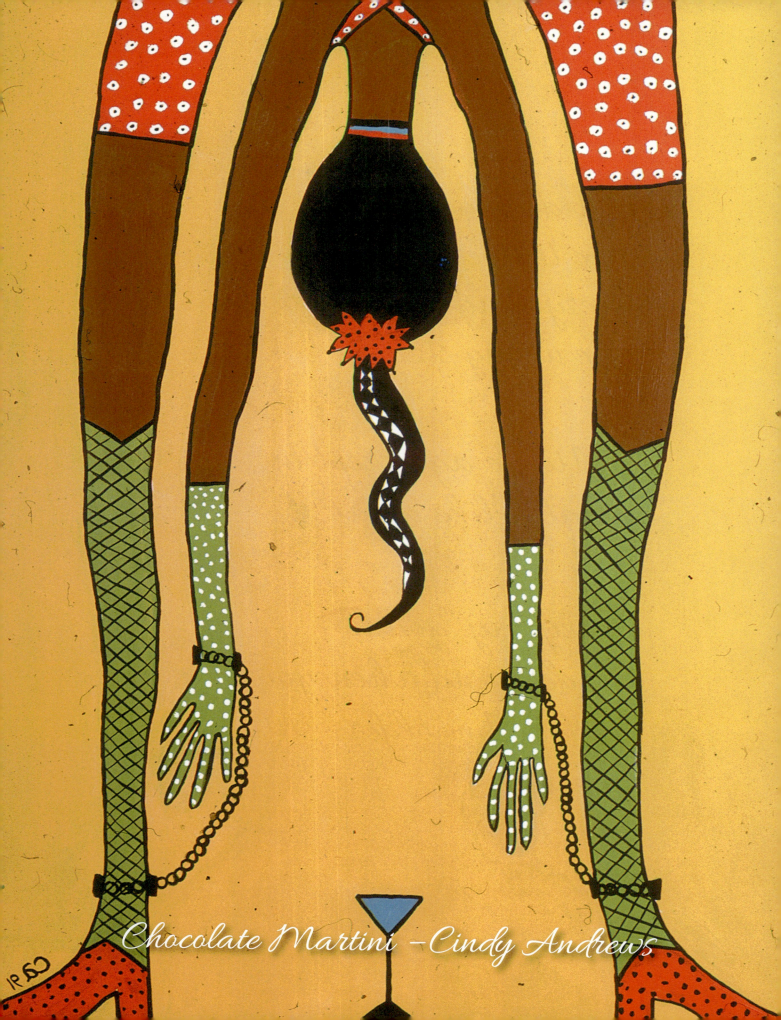

Chocolate Martini –Cindy Andrews

You must not strangle your future by loitering in the past.

Life gives you endless mulligans. Take them.

Manage conflict because life often gets messy.

Please stop talking; you're saying too many words in a row.

Don't let someone get comfortable disrespecting you. Decide what you deserve.

Youth plunges in where age takes time.

I would be remiss if I didn't recognize your continued crime of omission.

Unfortunately, derogatory is the new normal.

I hate to admit that indifference intrigues me.

My mind didn't wander, it left town.

Susan –Cindy Andrews

Elegance never goes out of style.

That was worth the price of admission.

Unsolicited advice is usually available.

Your compass needs recalibrating.

I'm tethered as opposed to fused, at this juncture.

Just because someone has not abandoned their post doesn't necessarily signify their willingness to be there.

Two Face Bitch ~Cindy Andrews

The false currency of
status will keep our culture
hostage.

Don't live in a bubble.
You will suffocate in
there.

Indulgent humanitarian
is my oxymoron. What is
yours?

Glory and tranquility can't dwell in the same house.

Occasionally I tumble over the edge of appropriate.

I like bite sized pieces of wisdom, they are easier to digest.

Still

You may learn many things
by mastering one.

Thoughts are free. No
scholar can track them.

Open your mind and close
your mouth.   Don't tell
people, show them.

At least you're consistent in
your inconsistency.

I am not stingy with my
emotions, although that may
be an extortion of the truth.

Lighten Up

I'd rather die of passion than boredom

Van Gogh

Be outrageous! People who achieve mastery have that ability

- Gita Bellini

The best way to find out if it works is to try it.

Do it well. Finish it properly and move on.

Eunice Kennedy Shriver

Emotional armor is necessary when entering the drama zone.

As much as I try to control the universe, it rolls over me without a qualm.

Accountability coach needed immediately, anyone else?

Nobody is that busy. It's a matter of priorities.

Irony... life is dripping with it.

Suit yourself, but perhaps I will convince you otherwise.

She's not quite a desperate housewife, just new to the reluctant game of domesticity.

Breakthrough

Knowing thyself, that is the greatest wisdom.

Galileo

Unhinge from societal norms.

Beg to differ.

Disrupt the status quo.

Delve

Show up. It's half the battle.

Human beings are so adaptable, it's truly amazing what we can get used to.

Reveries

You will never have greater or lesser dominion than over yourself

- Leonardo Da Vinci

Printed in the United States
By Bookmasters